Ee Ff Gg Hh

Nn Oo Pp

6 7 8 9 0o

Uu Vv

DISCARD

OUR WORLD
in
CROSS STITCH

Jane Greenoff

David & Charles

To my children, James Eric and Louise Estelle with love always

A DAVID & CHARLES BOOK

Copyright Text and designs © Jane Greenoff 1993
Copyright Photography © Simon Apps 1993
except photograph on pp16–17 © David & Charles 1993
Cover design stitched by Vera Greenoff

First published 1993

A catalogue record for this book is available from the British Library.

ISBN 0 7153 0068 7

Typeset by ABM Typographics Ltd Hull
and printed in Italy by OFSA SpA
for David & Charles
Brunel House Newton Abbot Devon

contents

how to stitch

Counted cross stitch is one of the easiest types of embroidery.

All the designs are made up of squares which you reproduce on your fabric as cross stitches. In the next section [page 6] you will see how to read a chart.

YOU WILL NEED

To work a design from this book you will need threads, Aida fabric 11 blocks to 2.5cm [1 inch] and a blunt tapestry needle, size 24 or 22.

Some stitchers like to use a hoop or frame when they are working cross stitch. It is not essential for this type of work. All the designs in the book were worked without a frame.

THE THREADS

All the stitched designs in this book have been worked in stranded cottons (floss). Each length of thread is made up of six strands of cotton (floss) and you usually divide each length before you start sewing.

All the cross stitch in this book is stitched using three strands of stranded cotton (floss).

It is a good idea to "organise" your threads. At the bottom of the picture opposite you can see what I mean. The threads are cut into manageable lengths [20 inches or 50cm] and looped on to a piece of punched card like the one illustrated. This helps to stop tangles and knots.

THE FABRIC

All the designs in this book are stitched on Aida fabric. It is made of cotton and is specially woven for cross stitch. It looks as if it is made up of squares, which makes the counting much easier.

All the designs in the book are stitched from the centre of the fabric, which means you actually get the design in the middle. This is very important when you are ready to frame the finished piece.

The material used for cross stitch does tend to fray around the edges, so it is a good idea to neaten the edge in some way. Either fold over and stitch a narrow hem or oversew the edge loosely. This stitching can be pulled out when the work is finished.

HOW TO START

Divide the length of cotton (floss) and thread your needle with three strands.

Look at picture A opposite. Bring the needle up at point 1.

Leave a short end on the wrong side [see picture E].

Cross the square and go down through point 2.

Come up again at point 3.

Cross the square and go down through point 4. Note the position of the needle.

This half cross stitch can be repeated as in picture B, which shows how to complete the cross stitch. As you work each cross stitch on the material, it matches one square on the chart.

FINISHING OFF

To prevent the loose ends from undoing themselves, you will need to tie them off as you go. It is better not to use knots as they cause lumps and bumps that show on the front when the work is finished.

After working a few stitches, turn the work over to the wrong side and catch in the thread left at the start [see picture F].

When you have finished one colour, tie off the ends in the same way [see picture G].

Picture C shows that the top stitch should face the same way whether you are working up and down or from left to right.

Picture D illustrates how to add the backstitch outline around blocks of colour.

Picture H shows how to find the centre of the fabric and position the first stitch in the right place. Fold the fabric in half and then in half again. Press it lightly and work a line of tacking (basting) stitches along the folds. This will mark the position of the first – central – stitch. When you have finished cross stitching, remove these threads carefully.

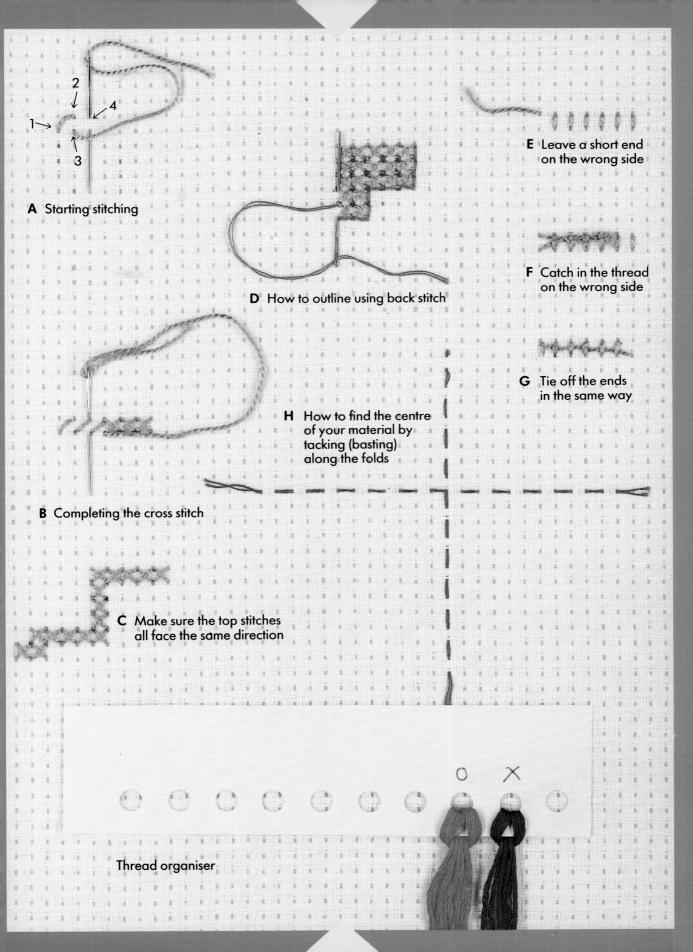

A Starting stitching

2
4
1
3

D How to outline using back stitch

E Leave a short end on the wrong side

F Catch in the thread on the wrong side

G Tie off the ends in the same way

H How to find the centre of your material by tacking (basting) along the folds

B Completing the cross stitch

C Make sure the top stitches all face the same direction

Thread organiser

O   X

how to read a chart

On the page opposite you will see a large coloured chart of the butterfly on a leaf.

This design is illustrated in the colour photograph on page 9. Full stitching instructions are on page 8.

The butterfly chart is drawn in felt-tip pens on squared paper.

Each square on the paper represents one square on your fabric. As we discovered in the picture on page 5, the Aida fabric used for all the stitching in this series of books is also made up of squares.

All the charts in the book are drawn in the same way. Each one has a list of the colours used next to the symbol in the key. The butterfly is made up of red, pink, two greens, yellow, lilac, brown and dark blue.

Each chart has the central square marked.

You can see that the first stitch on the butterfly is dark green. As with each project, the instructions for the butterfly show you where to start and in which direction to stitch. You will soon get the idea.

All the symbols are worked in cross stitch in the colour listed in the key. You can use any colour or brand of thread you wish, but if you want to copy the design in the colour photograph exactly, you will need DMC stranded cotton (floss). The shade numbers are included in each project.

The solid outlines around the stitching are worked in back stitch when the cross stitch has been completed [see pages 4 and 5]. You can see that the outline on the butterfly is stitched in dark blue and the leaf in dark green.

notes for parents and teachers

The pleasure adults find in all forms of needlework is often denied children today for all sorts of reasons. At school the needs of the national curriculum have left little or no time for children to experiment with embroidery. It is also a fact that many young parents were not taught needlework and are learning themselves!

Counted cross stitch is one of the simplest, least expensive and most rewarding types of needlecraft and is suitable for all ages and both sexes!

My own experience of teaching children under ten has been a revelation. The children concerned were volunteers after school hours and were mostly boys. After learning the basic stitch and how to read a chart, the entire group was designing and stitching in less than two weeks.

The most successful children were those whose first project was small and quickly completed. They were therefore eager to experiment.

I even know of one school who used counted cross stitch as a maths project. Surface areas were calculated, ratio and proportion were considered and percentages were studied.

HOW TO HELP

1 Choose small projects with large blocks of colour.
2 Select fabric that can be seen clearly and handled easily. Aida fabric is available in 8, 11, 14, 16 and 18 blocks to 2.5cm [1 inch].
3 Use blunt tapestry needles with large eyes in size 24 or 22.
4 Be prepared to thread and re-thread needles to start with. You may find it helpful to have a number of threaded needles ready for use!
5 Encourage the stitcher as much as possible, helping over any difficult bits. It may lead to hours of peace and quiet later when he or she is hooked!

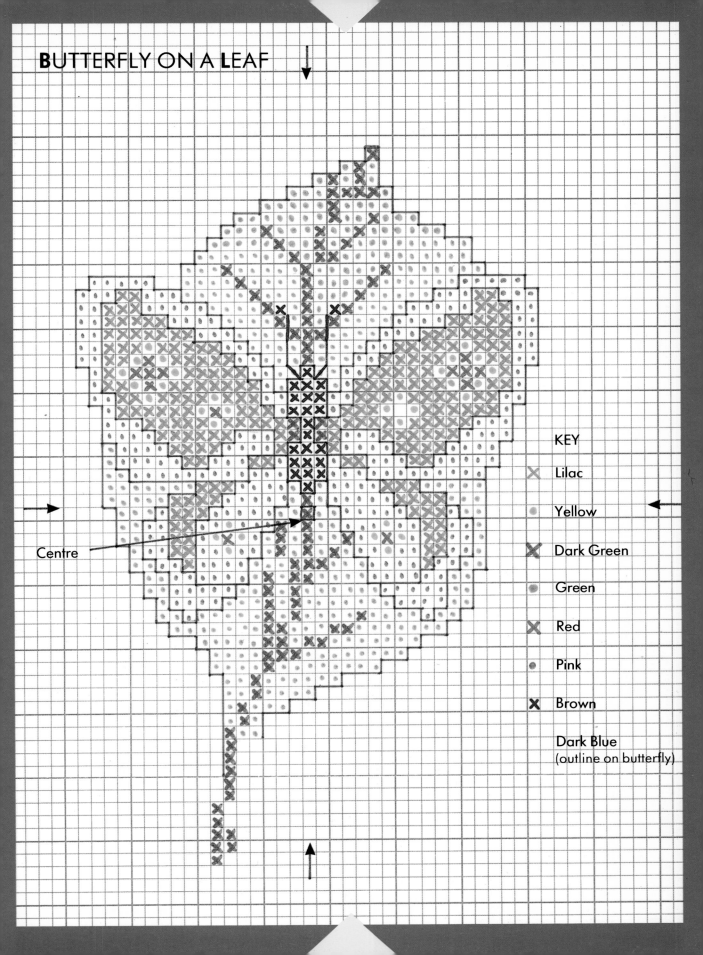

BUTTERFLY ON A LEAF

Centre

KEY

✕	Lilac
•	Yellow
✕	Dark Green
•	Green
✕	Red
•	Pink
✕	Brown
	Dark Blue (outline on butterfly)

BUTTERFLY ON A LEAF

CHART KEY

COLOUR	DMC	ANCHOR
Lilac	554	097
Yellow	743	0298
Dark green	561	0218
Green	988	0262
Red	304	047
Pink	602	063
Brown	898	0381
Dark blue	792	0123

STITCHING INSTRUCTIONS

● Cut a piece of Aida fabric not less than 18 x 22cm [7 x 8¾ inches] and hem the raw edges [see page 4].

● Fold the material in four, press and work a line of tacking (basting) stitches along the central folds. This will mark the position of the central stitch [see page 5].

● Thread your needle with three strands of dark green stranded cotton (floss) and look at the chart on page 7. You will see that the central stitch has been marked. Work this stitch in green

and continue to work down towards the stem, keeping the top stitch facing the same direction [see page 5].

● When you have stitched down to the "Y" shape in the stem, you can fill in some of the green leaf with the lighter shade of green.

● You can then choose whether to work more of the leaf or start the butterfly. You can turn the work upside down and work towards the butterfly, but remember to turn the chart as well and to keep the top stitch facing in the same way.

● Continue to stitch the butterfly, finishing off the ends as you go [see page 5]. Check for missed stitches, then remove the threads marking the centre.

OUTLINING

● Thread your needle with two strands of dark blue stranded cotton (floss). Add the outline to the butterfly in back stitch.

● Follow the chart and work around the blocks of colour as shown.

● You can work the outline on the leaf in two strands of dark green.

● Add the lines for the feelers in dark brown.

THE PLANETS

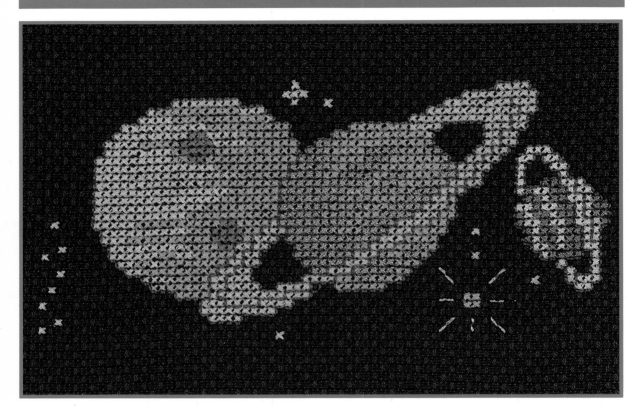

CHART KEY

COLOUR	DMC	ANCHOR
Blue	340	0118
Yellow	743	0298
Orange	722	0324
Pink	353	06
Red	304	047
Green	988	0262
Light Green	772	0259

● All the dimensions are given for Aida fabric 11 stitches to 2.5cm [1 inch]

STITCHING INSTRUCTIONS

● Cut a piece of dark blue Aida fabric 23 x 17 cm [9 x 6½ inches] in size and hem the raw edge.

● Mark the centre of the fabric (see page 5).

● Thread your needle with three strands of orange stranded cotton (floss). Look at the chart opposite and work the orange stitch marked as the centre. Work to the left, up and down, following the chart.

● Finish off the threads as shown on page 4 and 5 before starting another colour.

● Work all the cross stitch following the chart, using three strands of stranded cotton (floss) (except where one strand of pink and two of orange are mixed for the "distant" star). Remove the threads marking the centre.

OUTLINING

● The outlining is done in back stitch [see page 4]. Thread your needle with two strands of red stranded cotton (floss). Following the chart, work the back stitch around the cross stitch planets and rings. Then add the yellow backstitch lines to highlight the "distant" star.

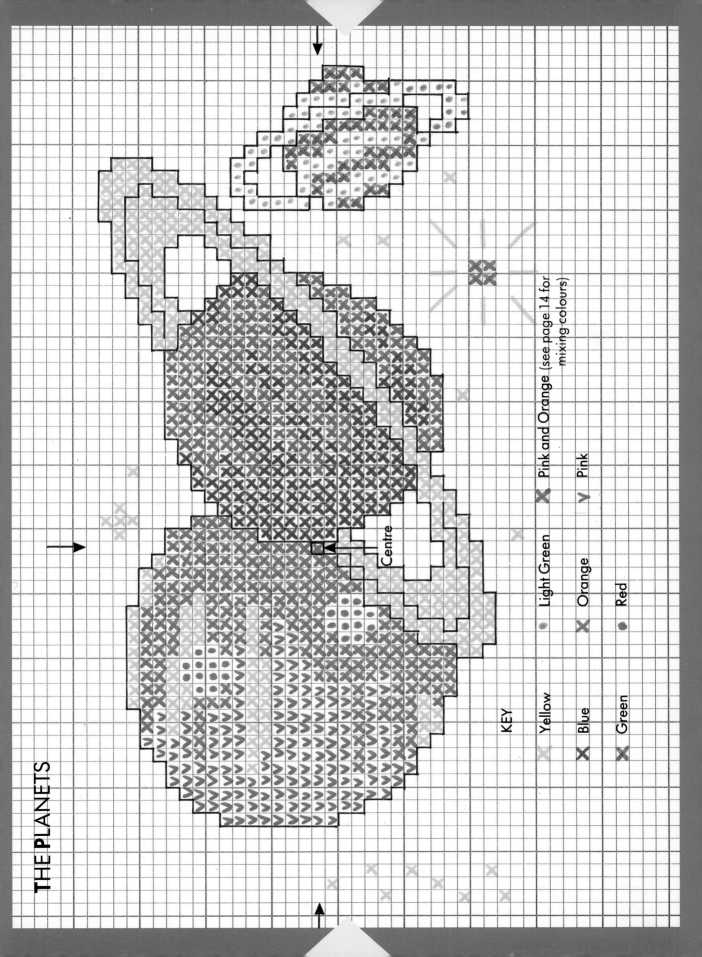

THE PLANETS

Centre

KEY

Yellow

Light Green

Pink and Orange (see page 14 for mixing colours)

Blue

Orange

Pink

Green

Red

THE WORLD

CHART KEY

COLOUR	DMC	ANCHOR
Royal blue	792	0123
Yellow	743	0298
Green	471	0265
Off-white	712	0926
Dark grey	317	0400

STITCHING INSTRUCTIONS

● Cut a piece of Aida fabric no less than 18 x 18cm [7 x 7 inches] and hem the raw edges [see page 4].

● Mark the position of the centre stitch.

● Thread your needle with three strands of royal blue stranded cotton (floss). Look at the chart opposite and work the blue stitch marked as the centre. Work across and down towards the coast of Africa.

● Work all the cross stitch following the coloured chart. When the cross stitch is complete, check for missed stitches, then remove the threads marking the centre.

OUTLINING

● Thread your needle with two strands of dark grey stranded cotton (floss) and add the backstitch outline around each country and the outer edge of the globe.

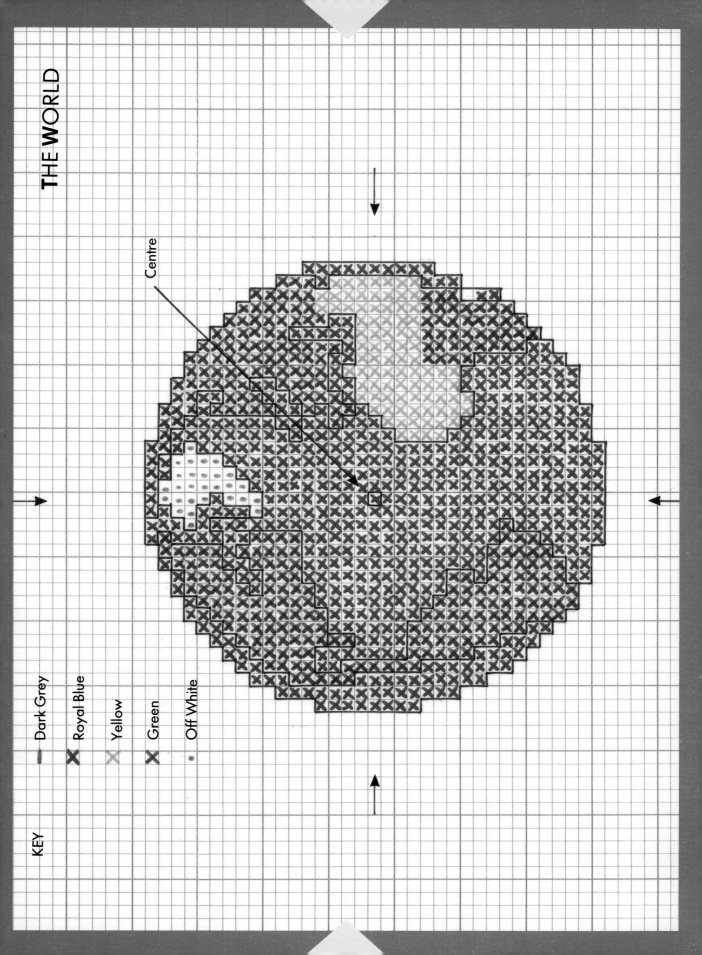

THE WORLD

Centre

KEY

— Dark Grey

✕ Royal Blue

✕ Yellow

✕ Green

• Off White

GIANT PANDA

CHART KEY

COLOUR	DMC	ANCHOR
Dark grey	317	0400
Black	noir	0403
Green	988	0262
Off-white	3033	0388
White	blanc	01

STITCHING INSTRUCTIONS

● Cut a piece of Aida fabric at least 18 x 17cm [7 x 6½ inches] and hem the raw edges. Mark the position of the centre stitch [see page 5].

● The central stitch on the chart is a mixture of colours. Thread your needle with two strands of dark grey and one strand of black.

● Work the stitch marked as the centre and continue with this thread mixture until the panda's front leg is complete.

● Thread your needle with three strands of black stranded cotton (floss) and work the panda's other front leg. You can now see clearly the effect produced by mixing the shades.

● Work the rest of the panda following the chart. When the cross stitch is complete, check for missed stitches, then remove the stitches marking the centre.

OUTLINING

● Thread your needle with two strands of black stranded cotton (floss) and work the back stitch [see page 5] around the blocks of colour as shown on the chart.

GIANT PANDA

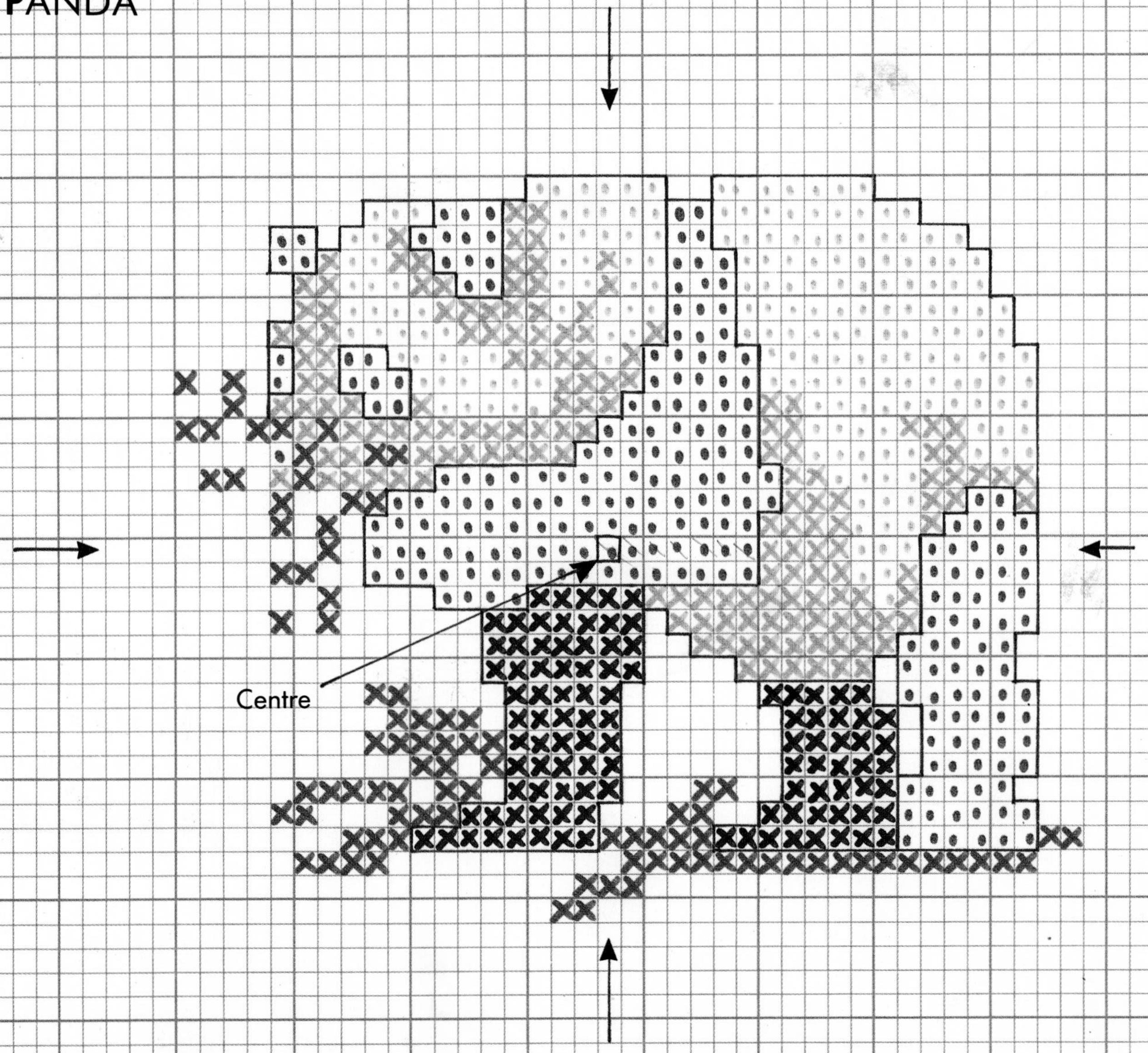

KEY

Black and Grey

Black

Green

Off-White

White

Dark Grey

Centre

GREAT WHALES

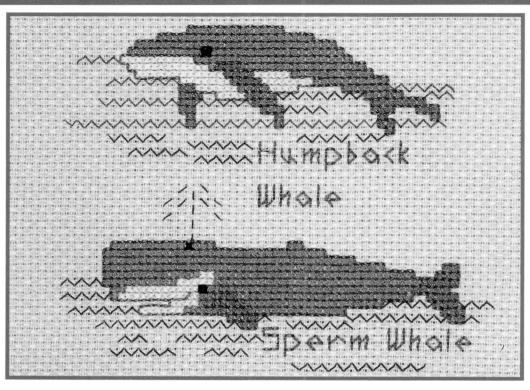

CHART KEY

COLOUR	DMC	ANCHOR
Black	noir	0403
Pale grey	415	0398
Dark grey	317	0400
Brown	640	0393
Royal blue	792	0123

STITCHING INSTRUCTIONS

● Cut a piece of Aida fabric at least 21 x 24cm [8¼ x 9½ inches] and hem the raw edges.

● Mark the position of the centre stitch as shown on page 5.

● Look at the chart opposite and you will see that the centre square is just to the left of the word "whale".

● Complete the Sperm Whale first and then count to the Humpback Whale from the water spout.

● Thread your needle with three strands of brown stranded cotton (floss).

● Count down from the central square towards the back of the Sperm Whale. Work the back of the whale, stitching across and down towards the grey fin.

● Work all the cross stitch following the chart. Then add the outline, the writing and the wavy sea. Don't forget to remove the threads marking the centre stitch.

OUTLINING

● Thread your needle with two strands of dark grey stranded cotton (floss) and the outline around the whale in back stitch.

● Using the same colour, add the writing in back stitch.

● To create the waves and water spout, thread your needle with one strand of royal blue cotton (floss) and stitch in back stitch.

● These can be done at random; you do not have to follow the chart.

GREAT WHALES

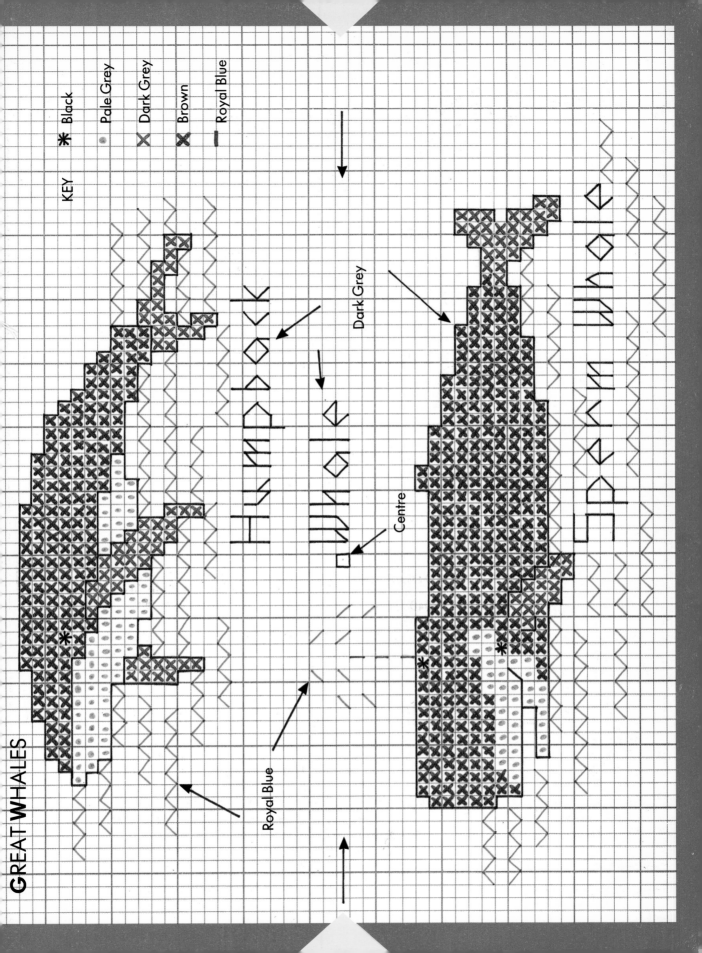

KEY

✳	Black
•	Pale Grey
✕	Dark Grey
✕	Brown
—	Royal Blue

Humpback Whale

Dark Grey

Centre

Royal Blue

Sperm Whale

RAINBOW PARROT

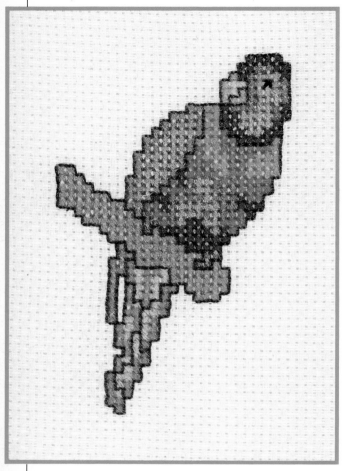

CHART KEY

COLOUR	DMC	ANCHOR
Leaf green	989	0261
Light green	471	0265
Chestnut	632	0379
Stone	640	0393
Orange	722	0323
Yellow	743	0298
Honey	738	0372
Dark honey	436	0373
Dark blue	792	0941
Light blue	341	0117
Medium blue	340	0118
Red	350	011
Flesh	352	09
Black	noir	0403
Dark green	562	0216

STITCHING INSTRUCTIONS

● Cut a piece of Aida fabric at least 20 x 16cm [8 x 6 inches] and hem the raw edges. Mark the position of the centre stitch.

● Thread your needle with three strands of chestnut stranded cotton (floss). Work the centre stitch marked on the chart opposite. Working across and down, stitch the branch on which parrot is standing.

● You can decide which way to work from here. Either work the parrot's body or his tail.

● When the cross stitch is complete, check for missed stitches and then add the outlining. Remove the threads marking the centre.

OUTLINING

● Thread your needle with two strands of dark green and work the backstitch outline around the bird. Outline the branch in one stand of black or chestnut.

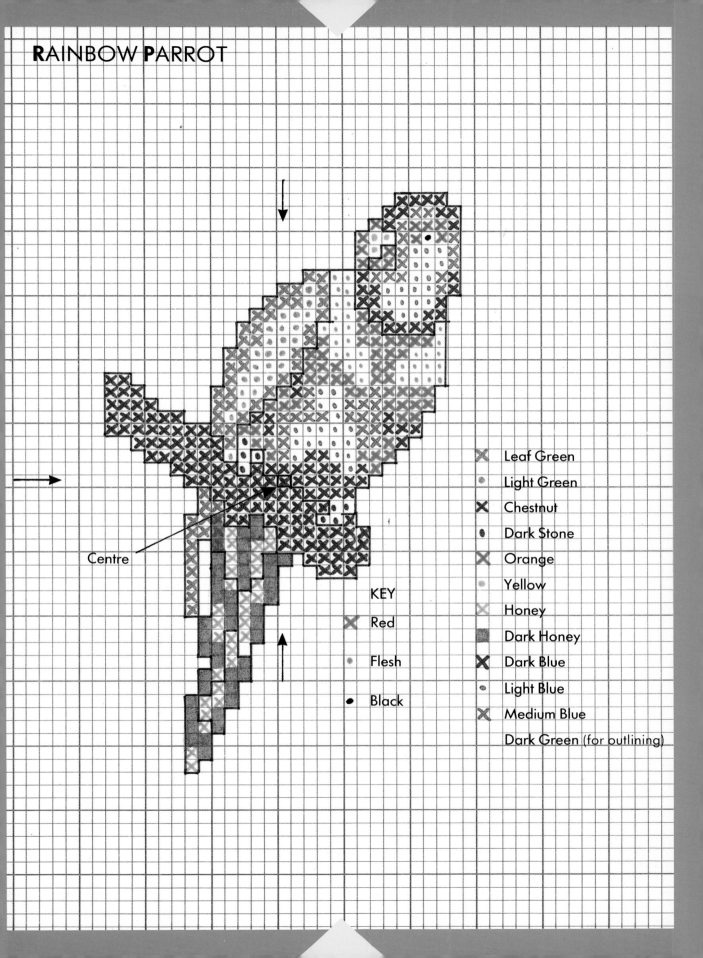

RAINBOW PARROT

Centre

KEY

✕ Red

• Flesh

• Black

✕ Leaf Green

• Light Green

✕ Chestnut

• Dark Stone

✕ Orange

• Yellow

✕ Honey

▬ Dark Honey

✕ Dark Blue

• Light Blue

✕ Medium Blue

Dark Green (for outlining)

ELEPHANT FAMILY

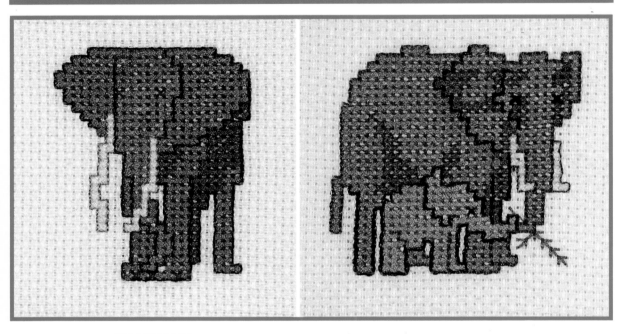

CHART KEY

COLOUR	DMC	ANCHOR
Dark grey	317	0400
Black	noir	0403
Brown	640	0393
Grey	414	0399
Off-white	712	0926
Green	562	0216

STITCHING INSTRUCTIONS

● This elephant family has been stitched as two designs, but could be worked on one piece of material.

● For the mother and baby, cut a piece of Aida fabric 16 x 17cm [6¼ x 6¾ inches] and hem the raw edges. Mark the centre as shown on page 5.

● Thread your needle with three strands of dark grey and work the square marked as the centre. Complete this small area, then stitch the baby elephant in brown. Complete the big elephant and remove the threads marking the centre.

OUTLINING

● Thread your needle with two strands of black and add the outline to the baby. Use black to outline the mother's ear, cheek and front legs. Use dark grey to outline the rest of the mother elephant.

● Use two strands of green to add the greenery in the mother's trunk.

● To stitch the bull elephant, cut a piece of Aida 16 x 15cm [6¼ x 6 inches] and work the design from the centre of the chart as above.

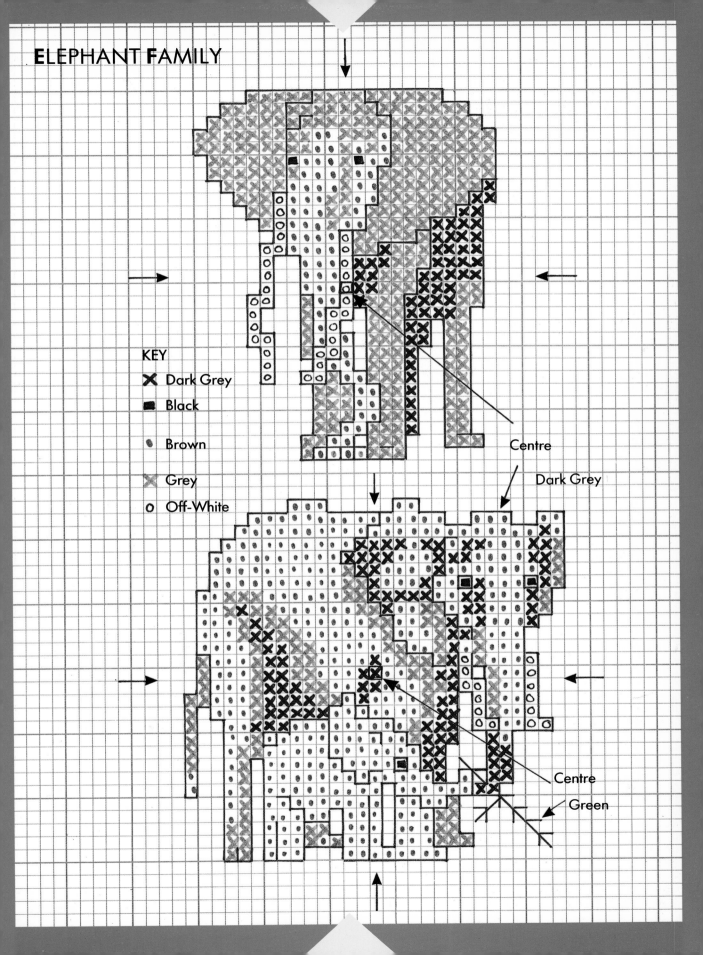

ELEPHANT FAMILY

KEY

✕ Dark Grey

◼ Black

▪ Brown

✕ Grey

○ Off-White

Centre

Dark Grey

Centre

Green

designing your own picture

This section contains coloured charts for you to adapt to use in your own projects.

The alphabet in the front and the back of the book and in the picture on pages 16 and 17 is charted on pages 28, 29 and 30, with the Chart Key on page 30.

The alphabet sampler in the picture includes a rainbow as illustrated in the colour chart on page 27. If you want to do your own version, use the lovely colourful charts on the following pages. The centre of each design is marked so that you can plan your own projects.

THE SNAIL

CHART KEY

COLOUR	DMC	ANCHOR
Yellow	744	0301
Pale grey	415	0398
Brown	640	0393
Dark grey	317	0400

THE TURTLE

CHART KEY

COLOUR	DMC	ANCHOR
Green	562	0216
Honey	738	0372
Tan	436	0373
Coffee	420	0375
Stone	640	0393

THE MUSHROOM

CHART KEY

COLOUR	DMC	ANCHOR
Brown	632	0379
Mid brown	407	0378
Flesh	818	0893
Honey	738	0372
Coffee	436	0373

THE CLAM AND FISHES

CHART KEY

COLOUR	DMC	ANCHOR
Blue	797	0133
Brown	640	0393
Dark green	561	0218
Light green	471	0265
Dark grey	317	0400
Flesh	353	06
Light blue	340	0118
Black	noir	0403
Light grey	417	0398
Peach	352	09
Red	350	011

THE RAINBOW

CHART KEY

COLOUR	DMC	ANCHOR
Red	349	046
Lilac	554	097
Yellow	743	0298
Purple	552	0112
Blue	797	0133
Green	562	0216
Orange	722	0323

MORE CREATURES – SNAIL AND TURTLE

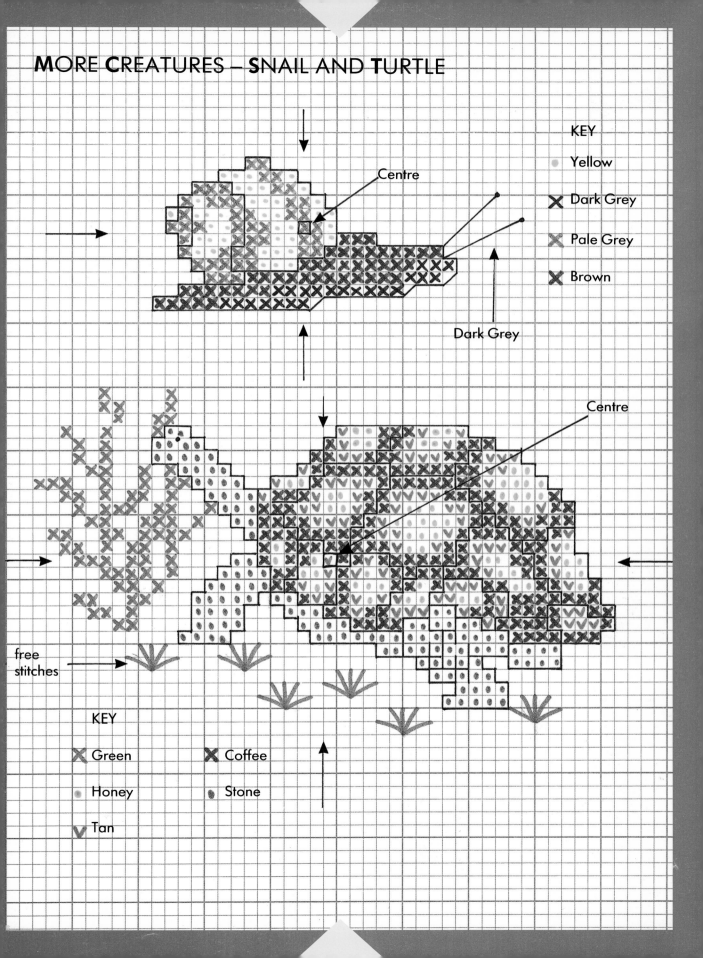

Centre

KEY

- Yellow
- ✕ Dark Grey
- ✕ Pale Grey
- ✕ Brown

Dark Grey

Centre

free stitches

KEY

- ✕ Green
- ✕ Coffee
- Honey
- Stone
- V Tan

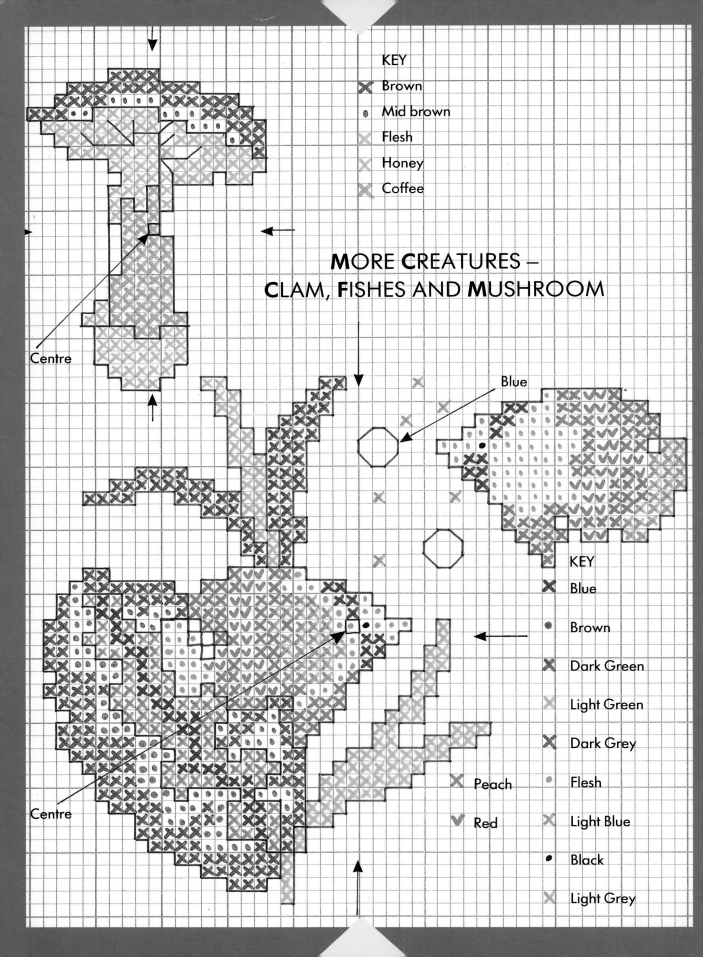

KEY

✗	Brown
•	Mid brown
✗	Flesh
✗	Honey
✗	Coffee

MORE CREATURES –
CLAM, FISHES AND MUSHROOM

Centre

Centre

Blue

KEY

✗	Blue
•	Brown
✗	Dark Green
✗	Light Green
✗	Dark Grey
•	Flesh
✗	Peach
✗	Light Blue
✓	Red
•	Black
✗	Light Grey

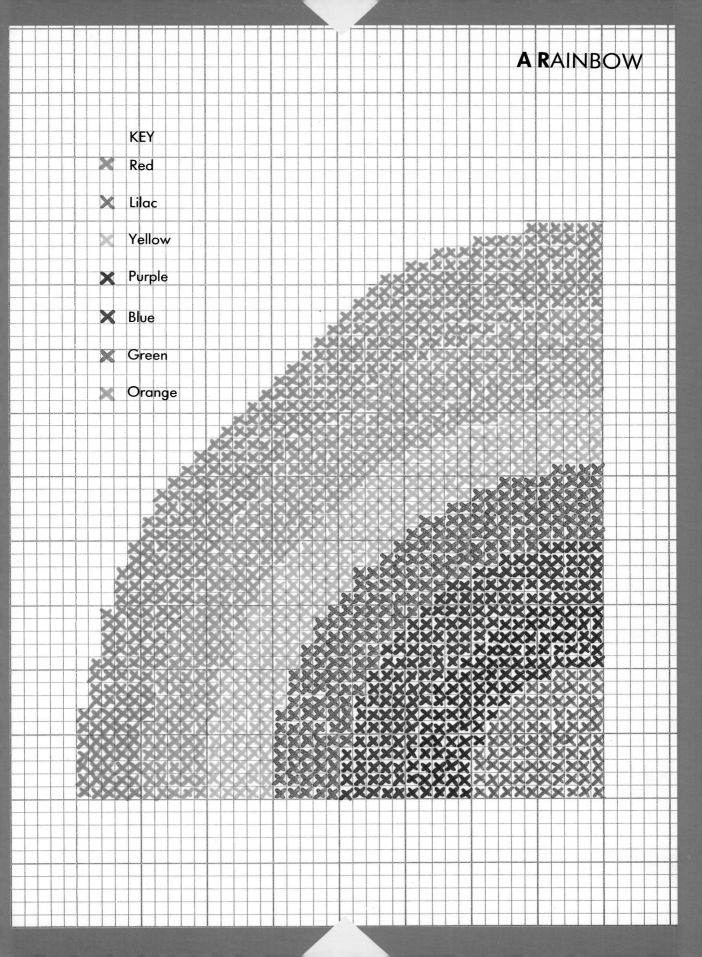

KEY

❌ Red

❌ Lilac

❌ Yellow

❌ Purple

❌ Blue

❌ Green

❌ Orange

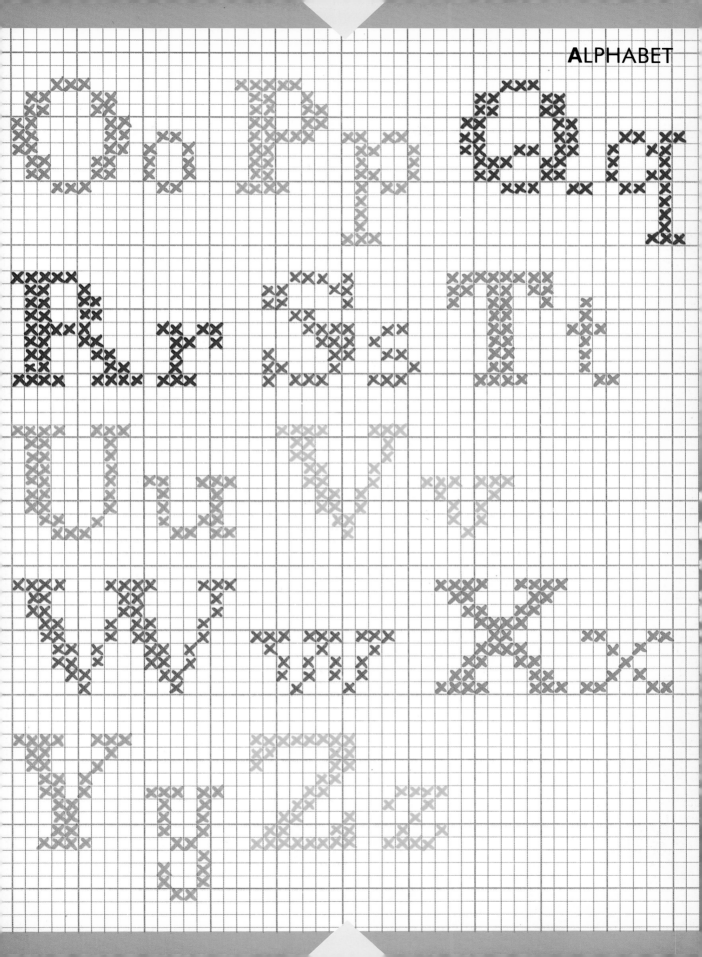

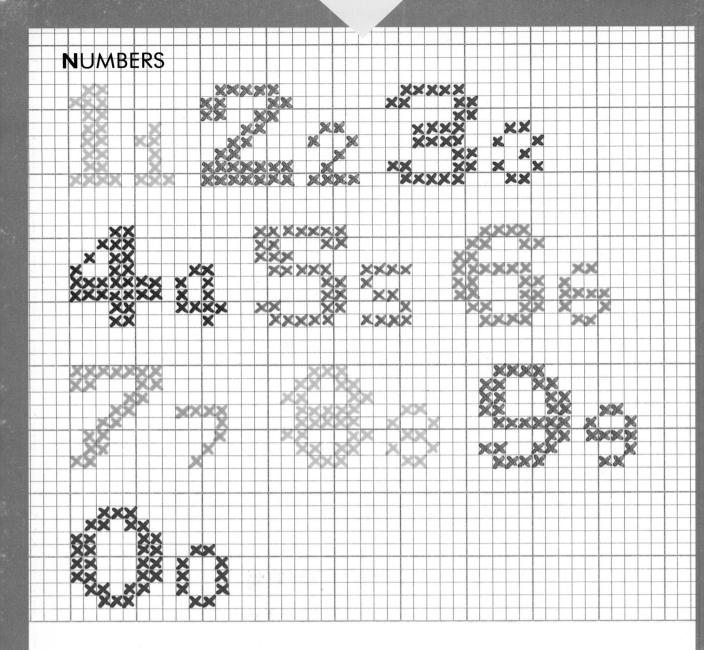

ALPHABET AND NUMBERS

CHART KEY

COLOUR	DMC	ANCHOR
Red	349	046
Orange	722	0323
Yellow	743	0298
Green	562	0216
Blue	797	0133
Purple	552	0112
Lilac	554	097

washing and ironing cross stitch

Here are a few simple tips to follow when you have finished a piece of cross stitch and wonder what to do next.

WASHING

Try to avoid washing your piece at all. Keep your stitching in a safe clean place, away from pets and worst of all, food and drink.

Even in the best-run homes accidents will happen, so it may be necessary to wash a piece of stitching. If you have used either of the brands of thread mentioned in the book, there is no danger of the colour running as long as you wash the item in warm water by hand. Allow the material to dry naturally and then press as below [do NOT use the tumble dryer].

IRONING

Before using a hot iron, check with an adult. Ask for help rather than burning your work or worse still yourself!

Heat the iron to a hot setting and use the steam button if your iron has one. Cover the ironing board with a THICK layer of towelling. I use four layers of bath towel.

Place the stitching on the towel, right side down, with the back of the work facing you. Press down on the piece firmly.

Cross stitch can be made into cards, pictures and books. You can experiment with your projects as you become more experienced. There are dozens of excellent books showing making up and finishing techniques.

HAPPY STITCHING!

acknowledgements

I would like to thank all the people who have made this book possible. My husband Bill, who continues to support my efforts when most would have moved out! James and Louise, my children who gave me the idea, and Vivienne Wells at David & Charles who believed in it!
Michel Standley and all the Inglestone Team who keep things running smoothly in my absence. Simon Apps for photography.
A special thank-you to the Head Teacher, Jon Allnutt, and to Beryl Booker at Fairford School, Gloucestershire, for all their help, particularly for lending me my team of advisers and stitchers without whom this book would not have happened!
My school advisers and stitchers were James Ktoris, Toby Brown, Michael Bowman, Sarah Grundy, Emily Whitehead, Sarah Compton, Steven Watson, Nicola Whiteman, Alison Martin, Natalie Doble, Charlotte Joyner, Lindsay Compton, Laura Hubbard-Miles, Lucy Scrivens, Jonathan Easey, Jennifer Easey, Rebecca Goozee, Jonathan Rishton and Kelly Benfield.
My faithful team of stitchers who stitch and check patterns, including Vera Greenoff, Tamsin O'Brien, Dorothy Presley, Carol Lebez and Hanne Castelo.
Cara Ackerman of DMC Creative World for the generous supply of fabrics and threads, and Tunley and Son for all art and framing supplies.

index

DISCARD

DATE DUE

JUL 7 2003	
JUL 0 8 2003	

DEMCO, INC. 38-2931